Praise for *Weird Fucks*

'Many early signs of Lynne Tillman's magnificent uniqueness are here on display: the deadpan humour, the wonderful telegraphic prose, the sure-fire wit, and a piercing anthropological gaze from which no one is spared. This first novella of hers is devastating and exhilarating in equal measure.' **Chloe Aridjis**

'*Weird Fucks* is brilliant, witty, economical, disturbing, delicious, devastating, devastatingly funny, surprising, revealing, reassuring, elegant, brutal, inevitable, cosmic.' **Harry Mathews**

'Weird Fucks. Killer sentences. This sex is hilarious, this sex is devastating, this sex is life. Lynne Tillman is the greatest.' **Charlie Porter**

'*Weird Fucks* is better than sex, it's a literary mindfuck, it blew me away...' **Stewart Home**

A catalogue record for this book is available
from the British Library.

Earlier versions of this text was published in 1980 and 1990.
This revised edition first published in the United States in
2015 by New Herring Press, and first published in the
United Kingdom in 2021 by **Peninsula Press**

400 Kingsland Road

E8 4AA

London

peninsulapress.co.uk

Printed in Great Britain by CPI Group (UK) Ltd, Croydon

2 4 6 8 10 9 7 5 3

ISBN-13: 9781913512057

Weird
Fucks

Lynne
Tillman

PENINSULA PRESS, LONDON

1.

THERE'S A SNAKE IN THE GRASS

I'm on my way, one of four NYC college girls, heading for Bar Harbor, Maine, to spend the summer as a chamber-maid, waitress, or piano player. Bar Harbor is on Mt. Desert Island, linked with the mainland by one bridge only and, we are warned, if there is a fire, we might all be caught on the island. Only two lanes out, they caution in dour Maine tones, and the only way out.

Bar Harbor is full of Higginses. There are three branches of the family, no one branch talking to the other two. We took rooms in Mrs. Higgins' Guest House. Willy Higgins, a nephew to whom she didn't speak, fell in love with me. He was the town beatnik, an artist with a beard and bare feet. He would beat at the door at night and wake all four of us. I'd leave the bedroom Hope and I shared to be embraced by this impassioned island painter who would moan, "I even love your dirty feet."

I was in love with Johnny. Johnny was blond and weak, his mother an alcoholic since his father died some years back. Johnny drove a custom-built racing car which had a clear plastic roof. He was a society boy.

The days for me were filled with bed-making and toilet-cleaning. I watched the motel owner make passes at women twice my age who couldn't read. We had doughnuts together at six a.m. I would fall asleep on the beds I tried to make.

At night Hope would play cocktail piano in bars and I'd wait for Johnny. Mrs. Higgins watched our comings and goings and spoke in an accent I'd now identify as cockney. She might have been on the front porch the night Johnny picked me up in his mother's station wagon. We drove to the country club in the middle of the night and parked in the rough behind a tree. We made love on the front seat of the car. I actually thought of F. Scott Fitzgerald. He asked me to put my arms around him again. He whispered in my ear that, although he knew many people, he didn't have many friends. He asked if I minded making love again. This would be my third time.

The rich boys who were sixteen and devoted to us NYC girls robbed a clothes store in Northeast Harbor. They brought the spoils to our apartment. Michael, a philosophy student and the boyfriend of one of us, insisted the stuff be returned within twenty-four hours or else he'd call the cops. The next night Bill returned the tartan kilts and Shetland sweaters that hadn't been missed. But he dropped his wallet in the store while bringing it all back and somehow or other the cops were at our door the night after. They spotted me as the ringleader. We went to Bangor for our trial and got fined $25 each as accessories. They called it a misdemeanor. The newspaper headline read Campus Cuties Pull Kilt Caper. I didn't really want to be a lawyer anyway I thought.

Johnny never called back again. I dreamed that Mrs. Higgins and I were in her backyard. I pointed to a spot in the uncut lawn and said with alarm: There's a snake in the grass.

A guy who hawked at carnivals wanted me to join the circus and run away with him. I was coming down from speed and learning to drink beer. Some nights we'd go up Cadillac Mountain and watch the sunrise. Bar Harbor is the easternmost point in America, the place where the sun rises first. I pined away the summer for Johnny and just before heading back to NYC heard that his mother had engaged him to a proper society girl.

2.

AN EAST VILLAGE VILLAGE ROMANCE

I was a slum goddess and in college. He looked something like Richard Burton; I resembled Liz. It was, in feeling, as crummy and tortured as that.

George had a late-night restaurant on St. Marks Place. I'd go in there with Hope, my roommate; we'd drink coffee, eat a hamburger. Fatal fascination with G behind the counter—his sex hidden but not his neck, his eyes, his shoulders. He called me "Little One." "Little One," he'd say, "why are you here? What do you want?" I'd sit at the counter with hot coffee mug in hand, unable to speak, heart located in cunt, inarticulate.

José was George's best friend and George had a Greek wife who was not around. The guys and I hung out together. $1 movies at the Charles. Two-way conversations between artists (they were both sculptors) while I hung, sexually, in the air. José had a red beard, George had no beard, just grayish skin in the winter. "Little One," he'd say, "what do you want?" He'd trace a line on my palm as if it were a map of my intentions.

Still, with so much gray winter passion, no fucking. Night after night, nights at the counter, count the nights. I met his wife who dried her long black Greek hair in the oven. They are separated. It is a recent separation and I am passionately uncaring. I am in love. I take trips with other people to places I can't remember. I spend hours talking with an older woman called Sinuway who gives me a mirror to remind me I am beautiful. She disappears.

José reminisced about the fifties when beatniks roamed the streets. In those days George made sidewalk drawings. One time José recounted, "George was very drunk—very drunk, heh George— and drawing a young girl's portrait. For hours and hours because he'd fallen asleep behind the easel, his face blocked by the paper. Remember, George?" Stories like these passed the time. Weeks passed.

George, José and I were in George's room and José put a ring on my finger then left the room. George and I were alone. He undressed me and put his hand on the place between my breasts. He undressed me in the doorway and fucked me. It went fast after so many weeks, like a branch breaking off a tree. The time had come. It was a snap.

"I want to write a poem," he said, his cock still hard. "Oh, I don't mind," I said, dressing as fast as I could. I wanted to be indifferent, not to burden him with my lack of sophistication. He had an ugly look on his face. Perhaps he was thinking about his recently separated wife drying her hair in the oven while he fucked a young woman.

Back at St. Marks Place I headed home, thinking this might be a reason for suicide. All that time, the perfunctory fuck, that poem he would write. It was all over. I phoned Susan who still lived at home; her life wasn't plagued with late-night restaurants. "What would you do," I asked. "Forget it," she said, "it's not important."

Later that night Hope and I went out again and I met Bill. He traced a line from my palm up my wrist all the way to my elbow.

3.

A VERY QUIET GUY

Bill and I left Hope and went to the Polish Bar not four doors from George's late-night restaurant. Beer ten cents a glass. We drank and drank; I told Hope I'd be home soon and wasn't.

Somehow we were upstairs in somebody's loft. Bill had red hair and brown eyes. He was very tall and wore a flannel shirt. We made love all night long, this kind of sleepless night reassuring. His rangy body and not much talking. He'd keep tracing that line from my palm to my elbow, the inner arm. He disarmed me. It was easy to do.

Early morning at the B & H dairy restaurant, our red faces like Bill's hair. Breakfast with the old Jews in that steamy bean and barley jungle. Romance in the East Village smelled like oatmeal and looked like flannel shirts. Our smell in the smell of the B & H.

George and José walk in and it was a million years ago, those weeks of gray passion and one snappy fuck. Sitting with Bill, so easily read, I smile at them. George looks guilty and embarrassed. I feel wanton and he is history.

Bill and I started to go together. He told me about his wife from whom he was separated. She was on the other coast. That seemed like a real separation. Bill was quiet and often sat in a corner. I thought he was just thinking. I introduced Michael, the first hippie I knew, to Nancy, my best friend. We spent New Year's together on 42nd Street, Nancy kissed a cop, the guys pissed on the street and Michael pissed in the subway.

Bill and I started a fur eyeglass-case-making operation which I was sure would catch on. We convinced Charley, owner of the fur store on St. Marks Place, that those scraps of fur would make great eyeglass cases. A fur sewing machine was rented and placed in the basement of the fur store. Bill and I passed nights sitting side by side, silently, in old fur coats, stitching up cases which never did get sold. Bill grew more and more quiet.

My father had his first heart attack. The subways were on strike and I took long walks to Mt. Sinai in my fur coat to visit my father in the intensive care unit. The first night he was in the hospital I couldn't go home. I slept on the couch at Nancy's mother's apartment. In the morning Nancy stood by the couch, anxious because the sheet covered me completely, like a shroud, and she wondered how I could breathe.

One night Bill fucked me with energy. Spring was coming and so was his wife, he told me later. I stormed out of the fur store, yelling that I would never see him again, and fumed to the corner where I stood, having nowhere to go. That fuck was premeditated— wife here tomorrow, do it tonight. I turned back and returned to Bill and Michael who said, "We knew you'd be back. You're too smart for that."

We went to Nancy's and suddenly I was sick, throwing up in her mother's toilet bowl. Bill held my head, my hair. He took me to my apartment and made me oatmeal. Left me propped up in bed with a pile of blankets and coats over me. Three days later, I awoke, my flu over.

His wife had a beautiful voice and was as tall as he was. And while I could get him out of my system, he couldn't get out of the system. He didn't want to resist the draft; he desperately wanted to pass the tests, especially the mental test. When he received his notice telling him he was 1-A, he tried to kill himself. Slit his wrists. Last time I remember seeing him he was sitting in an antique store, rocking, near the window. We waved to each other.

4.

NO/YES

I threw caution to the wind and never used any con-
traception. Nancy finally convinced me I might get
pregnant this way and made me an appointment at
Planned Parenthood. It was a Saturday appointment
and that night I had a date with John, a painter from
the Midwest, a minimalist. So the doctor put the
diaphragm in me and I kept it in, in anticipation of
that meeting. Besides, I had lied to the woman doctor
when I said I knew how to do it—I was afraid to put
it in or take it out. Let it stay there I thought, easier
this way.

We met at the Bleecker Street Cinema and watched
a double feature. Godard. Walked back to his place
below Canal Street. We made love on his bed and he
said, "I'm sorry. This must be one of my hair trigger
days." "What does that mean?" I asked. He looked at

me skeptically. It was difficult, very difficult, for men to understand and appreciate how someone could fling herself around sexually and not know the terms, the ground, on which she lay. He said, "It means to come too quickly." "Oh," I said, "that's all right." I kept comforting men. He fell asleep fast.

I awoke at three a.m. with just one thought. I had to get the diaphragm out. If it were possible and not already melted into my womb or so far up as to be near my heart or wherever diaphragms go when you're ignorant of where they can go.

I pulled a rough wool blanket around me and headed for the toilet in the hall. John awoke slightly and asked where I was headed. "For a piss," I said.

The heavy door opened into a dark hall. The toilet door opened, just a toilet and no light. I stood in the dark and threw my leg up on the toilet seat as shown in various catalogues not unknown to the wearer.

Begin searching for that piece of rubber. Think about Margaret Sanger and other reassuring ideas. Can't reach the rim. Reach the rim; finger slips off. Reach it, get it and pull. Can't get it out. It snaps back into place as if alive. Go into a cold sweat. Squat and try. Finger all the way up. Pull. Then try kneeling. I'm on my knees with my finger up me, the blanket scratching my skin. It seems to be in forever. This is a Herculean task never before recorded. An adventure with my body. In forever.

I pulled the blanket up around me and stood, deciding to leave it in for now and have it removed surgically if necessary. In a colder sweat I left the dark toilet to return to the reason for all this bother. I couldn't pull the loft door open. It seemed to be locked or blocked. I began banging heavily against the metal door. Hot sweat now. When John finally opened the door he found me lying flat out on the blanket, a fallen angel, naked at his feet. I'd fainted. He revived me and we were both stunned. "The door," he said, "was open." That's what they all say. He gave me a glass of water and we went back to bed.

The next morning, even though he said our signs were right, my fainting had indicated other signs. Signs and more signs. I walked toward Canal Street and a sign on the wall read Noyes Electrical Company. I read No/Yes Electrical Company. No/Yes, I thought, that's a crazy name for a business.

5.

AN AMERICAN
ABROAD

Rome was hot and strange in the summer. Nancy and I had been in Europe three weeks. We were tourists on the Spanish Steps. She met a Spaniard called Juan and I met his friend called Ricardo. Ricardo and I didn't get along very well and he thought I was an "egoist" as I tried out my college Spanish. All my sentences began with Yo and I was either tired, hungry or hot. Nancy and Juan began a five-year relationship that had her living in Yugoslavia for four of those years. Ricardo returned to Madrid.

Mao appeared one day at the steps. He was tall, thin and brown, a French Vietnamese. Suddenly he was my boyfriend and we were going to go to Greece together. Ours was a silent love affair and I'm not sure how we reached a decision like we were going to go to Greece together. My French was slightly worse than my Spanish, always akin to the pen of my brother is on... I believe we used interpreters, particularly when we fought. I discovered that I was sullen in both French and Spanish, but the languages, on my primitive tongue, seemed to lend themselves to moodiness.

Together, Mao and I did all the right things like eating in a poorhouse run by Franciscans and trying to get into one of the numerous movies being made in Rome. About fifty of us were taken on a forced march to a suburb outside Rome where Anita Ekberg or some other blonde star looked down on us from her balcony to single several of us out as looking like hippies. The rest of us were sent back to Rome, not right for the part.

Juan and Nancy wanted to sleep outside in the gardens of the Villa Borghese. Though I had a hotel room, Mao and I decided to join them. They disappeared behind a tree, some several yards above us on a small hill. Mao and I spread our blanket on the ground, took off our pants, made love and fell asleep. He was very beautiful and the lovemaking was nothing much at all.

It was a hot night and very still in the garden. I awoke, feeling light shining down on me. There are lights shining on us, the headlights of a cop car. Two policemen are standing at the foot of our blanket. They shine flashlights. Mao stands up pulling on his trousers. I can't find mine, they're hidden somewhere and I try to pull the blanket around me as my hand feels the ground, looking for them. But those Italian cops are fast, fast to spot a piece of ass. "Nuda, nuda," one yells, pointing at my ass as if I were already behind bars or in a zoo. My ass I figure is probably reflecting the light of the moon. I wonder if this image could ever be seen as romantic. The other echoes his cry: "Nuda, nuda." Now we're in for it, I think, semi-nude fornicating hippies found in elegant Borghese gardens. An international incident.

I become hysterical, nuda nuda, still searching for my clothes. I find them, put them on and stand up behind Mao, who is attempting to hide me from the cops. This gesture is futile and indeed ridiculous, as if Adam and Eve could hide from the authorities. They're not at all interested in Mao. I decide to play dumb. I point at my head and my chest, emphatically declaring, Stupido americana, stupido americana. I'm not at all sure of the agreement, but I figure they'll get the point. And the point is that if I admit I'm an idiot, particularly an American idiot, Americans are hated in Europe, if I admit all this, they may go easy on me. Mao stands by the blanket. They lead me to the cop car. I'm being taken away.

They push me into the back seat of the car. One cop gets into the driver's seat and the other tries to slam the back door after me. I shove my leg out so that he can't close the car door, unless he wants to cripple me. I leap out of the car and go running into the night. I keep running and the cops don't follow, they just get back into their car and drive away.

Nancy had watched from safety, behind a tree. Said it was the funniest thing she's ever seen. Like a Keystone comedy. Mao and I continued to communicate badly with one another until I said something which hurt him deeply—something I never understood, perhaps it translated poorly—and he left Rome, or so a friend of his interpreted.

Nancy went off with Juan and someone who called himself a friend of Juan's, seeing me alone, offered me his sister's house as hospitality. I fell asleep in the front seat of his Mercedes as we drove away from Rome toward what I supposed were the suburbs. I awoke in the car which was parked next to a field. After he raped me, he said, "Now we go to my sister's house." It had seemed pointless to fight him off and then go running around the Italian countryside in the dark when I had had a taste of what the police were like. He thought, because I hadn't resisted, that I liked it.

Two days later I got out of Rome, following the sun to Greece, hitching with a sixteen-year-old English boy who carried my rucksack on top of his. On the Continent, only, can one trust Englishmen to be old-fashioned.

6.

COMING OF AGE IN XANIA

I was sitting on a sidewalk in Athens, sitting on the curb in front of a shoe store. Jack saw me and called out, "Are you an American?" and I answered, "Yes," and told him I was looking for a hotel. "Share mine," he said, "a dollar a night."

Jack was from Chicago, a spoiled and wealthy Irishman who wanted to write. He had just gotten to Athens from Tangier. He had reddish hair, pale skin and eyes Carla would have called "sadist blue." He was recovering from an unhappy love affair which, having ended badly and to his disadvantage, made him vindictive and self-righteous. I didn't want to travel alone and he looked like a life-saver. We went to Crete and he hated me or at least it seemed that way. "Look, Jack," I told him, "you can stay in the house I'm renting but our being

together is insane since you criticize me constantly."
He didn't argue this point and we agreed to be house-
mates only. But Xania is a small city and a small Greek
city at that and a young woman doesn't leave a man
simply. Or at all. Friends of Henry Miller littered
the island and all would later descend on me for my
unfairness to Jack, who was drinking so much now.

I had fallen in love with Charles who arrived
with Betsy and her child. She was separated from
her husband. He had remained in their native land,
South Africa. Charles told me that he and Betsy were
friends. They seemed like adults to me, the big-time,
and when Charles looked at me longingly, I returned
the look. At first we were secretive. Betsy, who was
older and probably wiser, seemed to take this in her
stride and Charles moved out, into his own room near
my rented house. Jack still slept in my bed and every
night I would leave my house and go to Charles' bed.
He wanted to be a writer too. Jack and I would have
pleasant talks together on the terrace. We'd smoke
some grass and he'd talk about his broken heart.
Things seemed ok and in fact they were extremely
bizarre.

The first week in Xania I was cast, in my naïveté,
as the young thing who arrives in town and enters

a world she doesn't understand. This was my screen role in Charles Henri Ford's film *Johnny Minotaur*. I had been given Ford's address by a Greek called Stephanos. He approached me on the Spanish Steps, urging me to go to Crete and look up Charles Henri. He said Charles would want to put me in his movie. Luckily for Charles Henri who left Xania shortly after filming Jack and me in a classic beach scene—I wore a skirt and held a black doll in one hand, a pinwheel in another—he never saw his second heroine descend into her role.

Xania is made for secretive strolls, its lanes curve from house to house. I took these turns recklessly, leaving my house every night, strolling a curved lane to Charles' bare room where we would lie together on his skinny cot. Morning would come and I'd stroll back to my house. Breakfast at the Cavouria restaurant and a swim before lunch. I took to going fishing and the fisherman would smile as I walked down the pier to the tower and cast my line into the sea. I never caught anything.

Betsy continued to be civil to me. We went dancing at a taverna where the Greek sailors did their famous carrot dance. Charles didn't come and I sulked. Betsy was understanding and her graciousness made me uncomfortable. We watched a sailor place a carrot at his crotch and another sailor hack away at it with a sharp knife. I went to sleep outside the taverna in Betsy's car and woke to find Greek sailors peering through the car windows. I was driven home.

The strolls continued. Charles was good-looking, moody, given to short-lived enthusiasms and other things I can't remember. Jack and I socialized with Greek waiters. Waiters have always been partial to me—my mother has always said I had a good appetite. One such waiter took us for really good food in a place where men who looked like officers cracked plates over their heads, even though this was then against the law.

The waiter took us to his home and fed us some plum booze that's thick as a hot night. Jack and I went home and I went for my usual stroll. Several weeks later it was common knowledge that the waiter's common-law wife wanted to kill me. Alfred Perles, his wife, and Betty Ryan—the friends of Miller—all accused me of destroying Jack. It was the right time to leave.

The woman who took care of my rented, decrepit house and lived just across the lane offered to wash my hair and bathe me. I hadn't had a hot bath in two months. She heated the water in a huge black cauldron over a fire in front of her house. She sat me in a plastic tub. She even scrubbed my back. I felt she had some sympathy for me, and had watched, from her position in the chorus, other, similar young women.

There was no love lost. Charles slept at my house on my last night in Crete, Jack having sailed away, alone, almost nobly, a week before. I refused to make love with Charles, complaining of the heat and the bugs, and as a final indignity kept my underpants on and slept over the covers, while he slept beneath them. Charles and Michael, who had played Count Dracula in Ford's movie, drove me to the airport. On a similar ride one year later Betsy's husband who had come, I imagine, to win her back, would be killed in a car crash. I made it back to Athens.

7.

A PASS FOR THE NIGHT

Jos and I had been living together eight months, first in London and then in Amsterdam, where he and I ran a cinema and a film cooperative. He was in Utrecht visiting his girlfriend and I was in our room, wearing my Victorian nightgown and suffering. It was as if I were still taking speed—couldn't sleep, the night was ragged and endless. It wasn't easy to find sleeping pills or tranquilizers in Amsterdam. The Dutch were more into natural drugs, like hash. Later heroin.

Piet was a painter who lived just around the corner; he had been in a Godard film, was traveled, had a French wife who often left him; he was tough. He might have some pills.

I threw my fur coat over my nightgown. It was winter. In Amsterdam one can visit unannounced.

I put on a pair of old-fashioned shoes and headed out in the middle of the night. It was snowing, all white out, like my nightgown.

An American named Marty was with Piet. Both had similar reputations. It was odd to see them together. I had met Marty a week before on the night I'd received notice from Jos that he wanted to move out, that he wanted us to live separately. He loved me, he said. I knew from the love letters left on our bed that Jos was fucking someone else. This is the stuff that tries our souls. Oh, we hadn't been happy. I felt I was being finished off, planed down. After his phone call, I went, unhinged, to Cathrine's, where Marty happened to be. I cried as if I knew him or as if he weren't there. Cathrine handed me a joint. Misery became an awful joke. "Marty," I laughed, "do you know a man for me?" His response, and I can't remember it exactly, indicated he was a man. I couldn't understand why a man would want a woman in pain. I wasn't sophisticated about sadomasochism.

That was a week ago and here I am in Piet's studio with Marty, and I'm an inmate with a pass for the night. I kept on my heavy fur coat to hide my nightgown, which made my presence even more eccentric.

We listened to Dylan's latest album. Piet didn't have any pills, just hash. Marty said, "I like your shoes." It was an erotic comment, slightly perverse from his lips. He said he wanted to photograph me. I wish he had. I would have liked a picture like that, in the same way that I've always wanted to steal one of those US Post Office pictures of the Ten Most Wanted.

He stayed until 5 a.m. We fucked. I was a ghost. He left to return to his Dutch wife, to awaken in their bed. I didn't care at all. "Stay beautiful," he called out as he closed the door behind him. I stayed awake for several more nights.

By the time Jos returned I had accepted my destiny, the universe and his leaving our room. I wanted him to go. He didn't. And then I accepted that too. Marty, seeing Jos and me together, never flirted with me again, though we remained friendly. I wasn't sure if it was disinterest or respect for another man's territory. I didn't really care either way. I was the one who finally moved out of the room on the Anjeliersstraat (Angel Street). But that was not the end.

8.

LIES IN DREAMS

Breaking up is hard to do. After more than a year with Jos, I went alone to Paris and London. Jos followed; my parents and one of my sisters were in Paris but I didn't introduce them to him. He wasn't supposed to be there. I went to London and Jos and I lived together again, briefly, in that city until we had to find another room. Searching for a room in London proved too much for our poor spirits. Jos returned to Holland.

I met John at a film festival in London, thought he was an interesting man. He told me he was a poet and a publisher and might publish my work. Since I had no work to publish, I didn't pursue him. He pursued me. One morning Jos left for Holland and that night John was at my door. We went to see Warhol's *Bike Boy*. John's uncanny instinct for the kill would reappear, but not for another two weeks.

He would come calling and I'd never be at home. He'd leave word that he'd been. I became interested and sent a postcard telling him I was going to New York and Amsterdam but would see him when I got back to London. I was blasé. That night John appeared and found me. This moment having built to a fevered pitch, it was love at the front door. Then we had some tea.

I had not remembered any of our previous conversations, held at the film festival. He told me that we had had a long discussion about why I could not watch Otto Muehl's film *Sodoma* in which an animal is killed, and at the same time I was not one of those who wanted to stop Muehl from making a live action in the theater itself.

That second but first evening we joined my friends Susan and David for dinner and, later, a lecture at the Etherius Society. Got stoned during dinner and dropped a Van Morrison album from quite a height onto the record player after being told "one can do things better when stoned." This reminded me of that line in Djuna Barnes' story about her sister, "She sugared her tea from too great a distance."

The Etherius Society's leader was Charles King, a medium who believed himself to be in direct contact with the Venutians. The Society held its meetings at the end of the Fulham Road and in the basement of what appeared to be an ordinary English house. London always gives the appearance of the very ordinary. The lecturer was dressed in a business suit. John and I were in no ordinary state. The audience was mixed—old, young, artists, housewives and businesspeople. The lecturer spoke for two hours or what seemed a lifetime. John and I laughed without sound. Our faces were impacted with mirth and, though the lecturer glowered at us as he spoke about the Venutians and the Martians, we really couldn't help ourselves. It was when the tape of Charles King's conversation with the head Venutian played that some awful guttural sound came from me. "Come in, come in, Venus," King called. And the head Venutian answered, "Nim Nim two two, Nim Nim two two, I can hear you, old chap." The lecturer was furious now and John who was used to how ordinary English craziness is was able to control himself. The lecturer continued to stare straight at us and said, "We are now going to say the Venutian prayer. The lights will dim. And I would like to say one thing. You can snigger at the Martians but you cannot laugh at the Venutians."

And so we fell in love and that night slept side by side in a large bed while another man slept in another bed in the same room. We did not fuck. I felt we had anyway, that his body had moved into mine. And then he did move in. I met all the English concrete poets and learned to drink tea from morning to night. We invented Fluff, a kind of joke about how we were existing, which turned out to be our relationship. When we made love he refused to go down on me but wanted me to suck his cock. And when he looked at me I turned to lava.

I went to Amsterdam to tell Jos it was over. In true romantic fashion I did this from a sickbed; I'd sent him a telegram the day before saying that I was too ill to come to him. Jos came to me and sat on the edge of my bed for an hour as I spoke about why we couldn't go on. He was silent. (In the excess of my passion for John, I met another Englishman at one of Amsterdam's canals and we made love too. I threw away his telephone number and regretted this later.)

I returned to London and crazed days and nights with John. We shared a room on Lancaster Road near the Portobello Road. Our life was made of tarts, tea, cream and constant visits. One young man we visited, a poet, died the next year. His girlfriend later made love with John. I later made love with a close friend of John's. We all were trying to continue connections that had once been.

John wore a thick wool robe and I wore a Japanese kimono that was always open to him. My thoughts were Spenserian; I was the true love and even if I were to go he would know the false from the true. I went to New York and stayed two months, sleepwalking around the city, seeing friends, going places, possessed. Nancy hardly knew me. I earned money to return, and when I did, went to Susan and David's. They told me John had been acting very strangely. So I phoned him and he hardly said hello. The next day he phoned me and asked me to come see him. He told me he was encased in glass. We spoke for more than an hour. He refused my presents and presence. He had gotten very thin and cut his hair short; he looked like a monk. I left his room and spent two months, waiting, in a Victorian nightgown. Anyone who has ever worn a Victorian nightgown knows its meaning, it is the gown of an inmate. I took Valium and waited, would see John on the Portobello Road on rare walks out.

Over an Indian dinner a friend of his told me John was living with another woman. It was just after I'd bitten into a piece of food wrapped in silver paper. It was the beginning of the end of true romance, a fall that lasted two years.

I dreamed that I was with my father in my hometown. We are driving around the 20th Century Fox Estate. My father asks if I can settle down again and I say I don't know. Suddenly I am running wildly, wildly, down a wide path with trees lining each side. A man on horseback approaches and I leap out of the way only to hit a smaller horse, a pony. The pony drops to the ground. The man dismounts. My father reappears. The horseman looks very sad. "He's not dead," I cry. "I merely hit him." "No," the horseman says, "he's not dead, but he is blind. We'll have to shoot him." I scream.

I told John's friend the dream—he is the one I, woodenly, make love with in the future—and the friend said that there are lies in dreams too. I avoided speaking to people for a while.

9.

SUSPICIONS CONFIRMED

By now everyone knows that Valium is one way to get over a love affair. After taking those pills long enough, life becomes intensely fair: everything is the same. In this condition I visited friends and acquaintances with equanimity. Even people I didn't like. At one home I met Tim, a fringe Hollywood exile, actor and public relations person for something or other. He was also a photographer. I met him and went home without expectation of particular interest, this being one of Valium's cachets.

One week later the phone rang in the middle of the night. He said he'd been trying to reach me for a week, had even wired an office in New York at which he thought I worked. His enthusiasm only intrigued me.

He arrived with flowers and bought me steak. We got stoned and Tim called his friend Harold, a black Englishman who seemed to represent to Tim all that is cool and noble in the world. Harold invited us to his girlfriend's house outside London, and drove us in his car. I sat in back which was all right with me as I had become morose and paranoid. We were all very stoned, and I assumed we wouldn't arrive at the home of the ambassador from, I was told, a small African nation. Harold was dating the ambassador's daughter.

Sitting alone in the back seat of the car, I kept thinking that Harold was driving sideways, that the road was giving way at every turn, that the car might fly into the air. I distrusted Tim inordinately, and Harold was looking at Tim, and not at the road. Their laughter encouraged my worst fears.

We arrived at the ambassador's house and were introduced to his children. Harold's girlfriend was the eldest daughter. She led us to the basement which had been converted into a game or conference room. It was filled with six oversized leather lounge chairs. Like every ambassador's daughter I've ever met, she had been educated in a French convent. The four of us sat in chairs much too big for us. I grew more and more alarmed. I hadn't the slightest desire to fuck Tim but there seemed no way out. There was an inevitability about the night. I was being driven places I didn't want to go. The mode was ineluctable.

Harold drove us back to the city and dropped us at my place. Tim and I smoked some African grass. I stared at Tim, and he became recognizable. "You look," I said, "like my father's charcoal gray Perry Como sweater." He looked at me quizzically but still advanced. I couldn't understand why, I thought my remark was devastating.

Tim's stupidity was dangerous. When finally we were fucking, he was given to calling out, "That's some cunt. That's some cunt." In my condition his love-talk became absurd exaggeration. He made too much of a good thing (I thought). His enthusiasm grew as I retreated inside, and as if to draw me out, to reach me, he whispered bloodlessly, "I'd like to kill you with my cock." That was it. I knew it—in bed with a dangerous maniac who wants to kill me with his cock. All my suspicions were confirmed. This whole evening I was hanging on the edge of the fence, rigid with suspicion that was now given credence.

I drew back from his embrace and looked at his eyes which had narrowed. "That's horrible," I said, "I can't continue." It was impossible to prove to him that I was not crazy. The blind leading the blind and other such homilies come to mind. Besides I was in no position to argue.

It turned out that the wife I didn't know about was coming back from her vacation and I wouldn't have to see Tim ever again. When he left the next morning he gave me his sweater to keep.

10.

JUST AN ACCIDENT

I was staying away from men and lived and worked in Amsterdam where I found it easy to do so. A Dutchman let me use his back room and I camped there for the good part of a year. The Dutchman was depressed and cynical. I knew he wanted me to leave and, when Carla suggested I join her and George Maciunas for a trip around the Greek islands (George wanted to buy one), I had to get there. Jos found me some money, a six hundred guilder scam, and I went by train to Greece. Three days and two nights on the Athens Express in a compartment with a Greek man from Thessaloniki who fed me feta cheese, bread and olives. I read Jane Austen while on the train and feared that I might have to marry the Greek man, as several Greek women would pass our compartment and give us knowing smiles. I'm not one not to smile back and was relieved when he got off at Thessaloniki and I was not with him.

Carla and I settled again in Xania and she left before I did. I got very brown and into a little trouble, saying goodbye only because my money had run out. I returned to Amsterdam.

Jack Moore once said, "We are all going to be in Munich for the 1972 Olympics." I nodded, "Oh, yes?" and found myself there in the summer of 1972, along with twenty or more actors in Jack's theater company, The Human Family.

The hill of garbage, the rubble from World War II outside Munich since the postwar cleanup, is the site of the Olympiad. An artificial lake separates the games from the Spielstrasse, play street, where artists from Western Europe, Japan and America are to perform. The lake is polluted. The Olympics committee spent millions of marks to make Kultur at the games.

The Human Family was a participation theater group, using films, music, video and slides. I helped organize the production and directed some of the films. In Munich I also became a performer in the theater group, something I would ordinarily never do, having a horror of appearing in public, acting on a stage, but this was an extraordinary situation, more sur-

real than Meret Oppenheim's *Fur Teacup and Saucer*.
I wrote postcards to friends, extolling this quality,
and mentioned the thighs of the athletes.

The Spielstrasse abounds with German romantics
who never die. Every tourist has some piece of
equipment around the neck, arm or back. Busloads
of varying nationalities embark, disembark, to watch
theater pieces, clowns, conceptual artists, and then
cross back over the polluted lake to see the games.

The German romantic I met was called Karl.
He was political, did yoga seriously and ate macro-
biotic food. We spent several evenings in The Human
Family's common room. Karl whispered and blew in
my ear for three hours.

Our theater company performed every night.
The piece began on the top of the hill. We ran
downhill, each with a flashlight in both hands,
waving our arms in the shape of the infinity symbol.
I spent a good part of each day anxiously awaiting
the run downhill. Even with our flashlights on, I
was certain we couldn't be made out and I was afraid
of rolling down the hill. But my fear about rolling
downhill was small compared with what I felt about
jumping onto the stage and going into slow motion.
We were wearing overalls, too. Twenty of us in gray

uniforms. After moving very slowly, we were directed to stare out at the audience which should have gathered at the foot of the stage. From this bunch each of us was to choose a person to encounter and bring him or her up on stage. It was, for me, the worst kind of popularity contest. At the end of the piece we handed out donuts—the piece was also known as the Donut piece—and everyone danced around gaily to Shawn Phillips music written especially for the production. Our group earned the reputation for being very high, happy people, and often other Spielstrasse workers joined us for the dance.

Charley was one such worker. It took me some time to consider Charley seriously. Thinking in the midst of the Olympics, and while a member of a theater group that makes donuts its symbol, thinking was hardly possible. Charley just entered my life. He smiled a lot and so did I.

Then the Israelis were murdered, and everything stopped. I didn't know what was going on. No one did.

Charley came to see me. I was alone. The rest of the company had gone to the country. We spread all the pillows on the floor and lay down. The door opened and three members of the West Indian steel band—they lived rhythmically across the lane—walked in. We were both naked and the men stood over Charley and me. They seemed to have no intention of leaving. What with our group's easygoing reputation on the Spielstrasse, this might have been expected. We asked them to go, and they did. A few minutes later one came back and asked if he could be next. That's the way it began.

The Spielstrasse was closed because of the murders, "the political situation," as it was called, but the games were allowed to continue. All the theater groups and artists met to protest the trivial way in which Kultur was treated. The meetings ended in futility. The Japanese director Shuji Terayama and his group, which performed in costumes of black, red or white, succeeded in getting back on to the Spielstrasse. They started a fire and burned down their set, they burned everything. The flames could be seen for miles.

Everyone was going home. Charley asked if he could come with me to Amsterdam. I was surprised. Even more surprised when I discovered he already had a child, whose mother was a smart and crazy amphetamine-head. They lived in Paris.

We returned to Amsterdam and lived and worked together for more than a year. I hadn't lived like this for a while, and it was healthy to be fucking regularly. But Charley and I never did have much to say to each other. One day he came to me and said we shouldn't live together anymore; I lost him to a commune and his best friend, whom I couldn't stand to be around. It was hell for a couple of months and, when the hell was over, I rarely if ever thought of him again. This alone struck me as demeaning. A physicist once told me that one view of our universe is that its stability is an accident, that thousands upon thousands of relationships are unstable and that chance alone holds ours together.

11.

LEAN TIMES

Watching an English television play reminds me of life with Roger, an English actor I lived with for two months. Charley and I had split up, work at the film cooperative was impossible—no one cooperated. The book I'd finished editing a year before still wasn't published and into this hole came an English acting company. The play they brought to Amsterdam was adapted from a novel a friend had written and the author being a friend, the cast became friends too. Of course no one makes friends that easily.

It was Edward whom the author told me to look up, but I looked instead at Roger who was playing pinball after the play. It was, oddly enough, Valentine's Day. Two years before I'd written a short story on this day about the day and this year I found myself falling in love again. It is safer to stay indoors.

Three nights later Roger and I walked around Amsterdam, drinking in several bars, walking around and around, the way one can in Amsterdam, the city having been built in a semicircle. "Not tonight," I told Roger. We ended up at four a.m. in an Indonesian fast-food joint on the Leidseplein and ate peanut-covered meat. Shaslik.

Economics affects our life specifically: I had no money and no place to live since leaving the film cooperative. I had been living off the fat of the land and now, further into the seventies, there wasn't so much excess. Everything was getting tighter. After all those flowers and assassinations, optimism had died. Business went on as usual. Lean times. Roger had a small house in London and a rented cottage in Norfolk.

Our third night in Amsterdam we smoked and ate some hash. We took a walk and as we walked I felt we weren't getting anywhere. There may be no progress, but still I felt we weren't moving at all. Roger was staying in a small hotel, the one set aside for English actors when they came to Amsterdam. They came often—Dutch theater is lamentable. He said as we got closer to the hotel, "How are we going to get to my room?" The usual question of getting past the room clerk. With all the wisdom I could muster I replied, "We'll just walk up the stairs." Roger was amazed at this profundity, so simple, so direct, and indeed the way to his room was just past the room clerk and up one flight of stairs. The route to Roger himself was not so direct.

The next morning he left the hotel to stay at Mimi's house. I couldn't tell from the way Roger described Mimi and her situation if he was in love with her or she with him. In any case he described her primarily as a friend and an older woman, as if that would invalidate her. Later she and I became friends, and Roger's deviousness was reflected in phrases like "an older woman." It was hard for me to fuck Roger with Mimi below us in her solitary bed. The next night Roger agonized about whether or not we could make it with each other.

That Roger would leave town soon made our week intense, sweet. There's nothing like the promise of absence to make presence felt. When he left my bed to cross the Channel, Charley came to see me and asked me to live with him again. We could squat a house, he said. I figured his coming to me had to do with smell but he was two weeks late and I wanted to get the hell out.

Spring in London. I filmed Roger in Hyde Park and in the garden. I baked apple pies, wrote poems about making apple pies—rhyming pie with die—and took to watercolors again. What an interesting couple we made. We went to his cottage in Norfolk. Listened to Stevie Wonder on the radio and I wrote letters about cricket, actors, country life; my letters were shaped with Jane Austen in mind. She was my model for the genteel English country life. The English have got cottage life down, like having tea at four. We visited the neighboring Lord and had a discussion about tied cottages. The pound may have dropped as we spoke.

We returned to London. I took a job in the neighborhood, making twenty pounds a week for a five-day regime. And we shared the cost of living together. I continued to cook. Susan visited from Amsterdam and noted that she thought I was playing house. I was very serious when I played, though. Roger thought my friends were weird and I thought his superficial.

My book was up in the air and my plan was to return to Holland, read the proofs and come back to Roger and our routine life. Roger's heart, about which I heard a great deal, made it hard for him to be honest. He never wanted to hurt anyone. And while he liked me, he was still in love with the one before me. The day I left for Holland she moved right back in. Roger didn't let me know this, his heart was so big, for months and months.

I went to Eastern Europe with my sister, happy to be away, unhappy about Roger, again returning to Amsterdam. Roger called, after those months had passed, to give some apologies. Still later we held a conversation that clarified matters further. He thought because I had posed in the nude for a drawing course and had worked on a sex paper, he thought I would introduce him to the mysteries.

12.

GOING TO PARTIES

Living in New York City and going to parties. The last ritual, attending parties. Kathy introduces me to Scott who is kneeling and I kneel too. My knees begin to hurt and I stand over him. I'm sure he's queer with his Lou Reed hair, overalls and big glasses. I watch him dance. Not bad. I lose everyone I know and Scott and I begin to dance. He's very tall and I can't see his face which is hidden anyway by his glasses. The masked man. A bad song comes on and we lean against the wall. "Let's go to my place," he says, "and we'll come back in a little while. It's real close." That's friendly, I think, and say ok and off we walk in an area unfamiliar to me. His loft is farther than a few blocks and it's raining. Maybe he's not homosexual.

The loft is six flights up and I begin by bounding the stairs two at a time. "Take it easy," he says, "there's a lot more." I enter the loft panting. My eyes are attuned to small Dutch quarters and the amount of space he has makes us both look small, insignificant.

Scott turns on The Wailers and we continue dancing. It's that movie when the dance becomes The Dance. He says, "You were making eyes at me." I tell him I wear glasses. We're lying on the bed. By now I realize he's heterosexual and this is the fashion. "Are you Kathy's boyfriend?" I ask, suddenly. "Not anymore," he says, "we're both hot to trot." I'm not sure what anything means and insist, drunkenly, that we go back to the party. He thinks I'm upfront. "Since we're not going to fuck," he says, "wanna see my sculpture?" And next find myself seated inside a vibrating box.

Everything seems funny. I feel both innocent and wild. "Hey, little girl, you don't have to hide nothing no more. You haven't done nothing that hasn't been done before." Kathy walks up to me, "you've been with Scott?" "Yes," I say, "what about it?" She clears the decks and not only clears them but also indicates she has aimed me at him. "He's a good fuck," she says, and walks off. Is he or am I being passed on? There's something bloodless in the modern age.

Scott watches the discussion and says, "I coulda hit you for talking to Kathy." "Look, it's funny, Scott, don't you see?" We're dancing again, nearer to the wine and a Puerto Rican woman who really dances and I dance with her and smoke some grass and get given hash and Scott walks up and says (again), "Let's go."

We do the same walk, in the same night, up all those stairs, but there's a difference. "Harder this time," he says. Of course, I think. His roommate is at the far end of loft. I know he's here but can hardly see him. More California wine and the television on by our heads. My head is turned toward it but I am not watching. Pulling off our clothes, on the bed, he thinks I'm watching the movie. I am and I'm not. It's just on, a forties movie, and it fits right in, somehow, with everything else. The guy at the far end of the loft is snoring. Scott and I are fucking. "Did you come?" he asks. "Not this time," I answer. "Next time," he says. "I trust you," I say. But I can't sleep. The wine, grass and sex. Parched throat. Water. Need water. "Get me some too," he says.

It's dark and I take the long walk down the naked loft. That naked walk to get a glass of water. For a piss, or for water, so familiar in unfamiliar territory. Don Juan should see me now, gait of the warrior in a New York City loft. I find everything and return carrying two full glasses of water. I hand one to Scott.

Cold water hits him in the face and he thinks I did it purposely. "You bitch," he says, just like in a forties movie. Then I know. He wants that. He keeps calling me Bitch. There's something refreshing about this reversal: a masochistic man. "No," I say, "I wouldn't do that, pour cold water on you in bed."

He's fast asleep. I can't sleep. Why can they always sleep? Are men better sleepers? The windows bang heavy during the night. The rain bangs against the windows. I look at Scott, closely now. No hair, no glasses. He looks like a little baby and has a small mouth. By the light of the storm, he looks like an alien. A young alien. I have to stop this and sleep. I know more about his cock than his face. Big cock, small mouth. The sun is coming in through the windows and I'm watching it. The light is dark as the rain continues.

In the morning Scott tells me he's into being macho. "How do you mean?" I ask. "Well," he says, "it's sort of feminism for men." I tell Scott I have an appointment, which seems like a lie but isn't. With whom he asks. Sally, I say. Sally Blank? he is incredulous. Yes I say. "She's a good fuck," he reports. "This is just like high school," I say. "Oh," he goes on, "and you don't know all of it. Anyway, Kathy is

using this material for her novel. She uses the gossip."
At least that isn't new. He calls me bitch again as I dress
and then he undresses me and my belt buckle makes
a clumsy sound in the big, empty room. "Why didn't
you start this before I got dressed?" I ask. "You moved
too fast," he says. His big hand touches, hardly touches
my cunt, and we fuck again, not drunk or stoned. Lots
of light now. "You feel so good," he says, "and I have
to piss." He gets out, gets up and goes to piss. Stay for
pancakes? Can't I say.

He walks me to the door wearing a terry cloth robe
that just barely covers his tight ass. Lifts me high,
kisses me and unlocks the door. It's pouring outside.

Some months later, we've remained friends. Scott
asks how he can meet a woman. "I'm confused," he says.
"That's it," I say. "What?" he asks. "That. Just let her see
you're vulnerable. It works every time. Women are
suckers for sensitive men." The advice works. I'm invited to his loft dancing-wedding party a year later.
The bride and groom wear dark colors and both have
closely cropped hair.

13.

THE FOURTH OF JULY

I should have known better. Upper middle class guys from Westchester are trouble and can't fuck. But look at that I say to myself, he's in therapy, talks about his mother with affection, wants to know something about me. The modern man aware of female independence. I'm not attracted to him though he's handsome in a way I find reprehensible—slick, well-dressed, clean but sweats a lot. Still he's so normal. The bait taken, Josh beat at my conditioned barriers and I let him in.

It's my first Fourth of July in the USA in seven years. And it's the Bicentennial at that. I'm not sure what people are celebrating but Americans like parties. We watch fireworks from a roof on Canal Street. The approach to the roof is the most dangerous aspect on this pacific evening. For while Amy had predicted bombs and dutifully warned Sidonie, a French friend, to stay off the streets, five million people walk around Lower Manhattan, watch the tall ships, and eat. I eat Polish sausage and drink German beer.

The party begins tentatively as most do. But it is the Fourth of July and people want to have a good time. The dancing starts slowly and builds up, people secreting into the group one by one, then two by two. Martha knocks herself out on this hot night doing an energetic lindy then disappears. A man with a moist face approaches me from behind and asks me to dance. There's something about being asked to dance that takes me back to sixth grade parties. Being asked to dance in this way and by a stranger is so American and perfectly right for the Fourth of July. He's sweating which keeps me at arm's length until he asks serious questions which soften me to him. I dance with him for a while but dismiss myself graciously, saying I'm going to the bathroom. I want to find Sidonie and see if she'd be interested in this earnest man, in Josh.

Red, white and blue chalk marks are drawn on my forehead. It's not the mark of Cain but still one can't help making an association like that. Judy has lines over her mouth, more like a clown. Things seem to be heating up with old lovers walking in and out, the party filling democratically with people one wants and one does not want to see. I introduce Sidonie to Josh but she's not interested and neither is he. It's not that easy. We dance again and he leaves, giving me a kiss on the cheek and the ritualized "I'll phone you."

Patsy and I do a vicious dance, a tango of sorts; the time is right for dancing in the streets and movements such as these. I tell Scott that this week he is not one of my favorite people and he takes this seriously, so we don't speak for months.

Firecrackers keep popping off and everything feels slightly evil. For the urban dweller whose adventures are limited to sexual ones, the Fourth of July has nothing to do with America's independence. One's own independence is severely circumscribed anyway. We play out the hunt we can.

Josh phones two nights later when I had all but forgotten him. His voice is reassuring and certain. We meet the next night at a Chinese restaurant, joined by Martha and her friend Don. Martha and Don are blond and fairskinned, Josh and I are dark-haired and tan.

Alone in a bar we talk familiarly about recent problems and the women he used to live with. This is the usual fare. I am still not attracted to him but consider this my failing. I tend toward men who aren't as nice. He says, "But we haven't talked about your writing."

And he walks me home and since I have not changed my feelings toward him, I don't want him to go out of his way for me. He insists that he is doing what he wants to do. This kind of statement comes right out of therapy and I recognize it—he's taking responsibility for his actions. Still, he strikes me as sensible. We walk to my street near Wall Street, talking all the way, and he invites me to a party the next night. By now he knows I'm leaving for San Francisco in a few days. This has created for him an urgency to see me more. I don't distrust this. I ask if I can bring Sidonie to the party and he says, "Yes, of course."

The party is on the Bowery. We pass alcoholics fighting over shoes. Across the street from his friend's party, there is a fire in a flophouse. It's like leaving a war zone when we enter the party. The men and women are spotless and fashionable and they are artists. Lots of good food and drink. The discrepancy can be watched, like a movie, out the window. A few drinks and I begin to appreciate Josh because he is so very attentive. This is a form of flattery that is most convincing, particularly at a party. When I was fourteen I discovered that boys would fall in love with

me if I listened to everything they said. A strong sense
of integrity prohibited me from continuing this form
of seduction. And, in addition to integrity, there was
the problem of having to continue to listen to them.

We dance and I still don't want to make love with him.
I get drunker in order to overcome my disinclination,
even disgust at the prospect. I am sure I don't want him
because he's so nice, is like the boys I grew up with,
and so openly likes me. I feel trapped. And it's kind
of comfortable.

We return to his loft and I see his paintings, which
are done on the back of the canvas. This interests
me because it is in sharp contrast to his regular guy
demeanor. "You're less open than you appear," I say to
him, surprising him with this insight. I immediately
forget it, as if it were only academic, and sit on the
couch beside him. Noticing my reluctance he thinks
I'm nervous about making love with him for the first
time. This amuses me inwardly but I cannot share
my amusement with him. He begins to talk about
"the situation" and I know I'll either do it or I won't
so I say, "Let's go to bed." A lot of performers get on
the stage like that, just jumping on. Besides, I think
to myself, this is an act I know with and without
feeling. I am trying to get over a reluctance, the

reason for which I do not know. The mechanics of sex make it easier for a woman to betray herself, which leads perhaps to her having different feelings about sex from a man whose sex organ is always a sign. We make love and once it's over I feel relieved, like having gone to the dentist and just having one cavity.

When we awaken in the morning, I feel like talking, not rushing from his bed. By this time I'm involved— in something. Uninspired sex can win a masochist. It certainly makes sex not at all central to the relationship; it's so easy to forget. And so I felt that I really liked him and was not just attracted to him. Here is Puritanism, liking someone because the sex is bad.

I'm excited about leaving New York and having met a nice guy I can introduce to my friends. So I introduce Josh to lots of my friends, feeling certain and calm. He says I can phone him collect whenever I want. He phones me every week I'm away and I send romantic cards. I'm away for five weeks and don't make love with anyone else, partly out of this strange loyalty I develop like a rash when rubbed by certain kinds of men, partly because San Francisco didn't abound with men I could make love with. This combination appeared to be fate. Fatal.

When I get back to New York City, it is still hot. I phone him, leaving a message on his machine. He calls later and we meet that night. Everything seems to be going as it should. But he can't get it up. Says he is anxious about a show coming along faster than he expected. There's nothing to do about impotence except be understanding. But it was awful and not at all like the dream I had of my return to New York—he had made a painting that, when shot with a water pistol, moved in mysterious ways often called orgasmic.

We both bury the lack of lovemaking as if it's just one of those things. Josh asks me to go to the Hamptons with him for the weekend but when I phone the next day to find out when we're leaving, he begs off, and says he wants to be alone. That he'll call me when he returns. Says there's nothing wrong between us.

Sunday night passes, and Monday, it could've been a long summer weekend. Josh never calls and I am the one, finally, to call him. He speaks to me as if I were a foreigner, a greenhorn who has the wrong expectations about America.

One year later he comes up to me in a bar and, smiling, asks, "How are you and what are you up to now?"

I look at him blankly and answer "The same." "You're distant," he says to me, surprised, even hurt by my disdain. He hadn't been a one-night stand, a temporary shelter like a glassed-in bus stop on a busy, rainy city street. Anonymous and more or less alienating, or sexy, depending upon one's mood. He had attenuated the one-night stand into something more difficult to get over. For a while I was meaner in the clinches, not so easy to fool. There are some things I just won't forgive.